T0056471

Giuseppe Verdi
and The Golden Age
of Italian Opera

for Trumpet or Flugelhorn and Orchestra

6857

Aside from my adoration of his sublime melodies it almost felt incomplete to not include an aria by the Master of Salzburg since he favored opera over all musical forms. Before we begin discussing each piece, I'd like to mention to newcomers and remind those of you that purchased my earlier opera MMOs that the orchestral accompaniment tracks were recorded in Eastern Europe, specifically Bulgaria where they tune to higher than A = 440. Don't be surprised if you have to push your tuning slide farther in than ever before. The provided Bb tuning notes are tuned slightly higher, but I recommend you listen carefully to each track for there will be some variation.

The other thing to be aware of is that the accompaniment recordings contain rubato passages, ritardandos, cadenzas and fermatas which can be a challenge to get in sync with. Without the advantage of a conductor following your lead or a click track, multiple listenings of my renderings and the minus version for those passages is crucial to avoid frustration.

Also, in order to acquire an overview of the particular aria that you are undertaking, I heartily recommend that you go to YouTube and listen to performances by famous opera singers.

That said, we're ready to play Verdi's **Volta la terrea** (That tense countenance) from *Un Ballo Maschera* (A Masked Ball) a dynamic coloratura soprano aria. It's an exquisite piece and aside from the obvious tricky, out of tempo passages, a shoe-in for the trumpet.

Before moving on to Donizetti's **Quando rapito in estasi,** I suggest you go to YouTube and listen to an incredibly inspiring performance by Dame Joan Sutherland as Lucia di Lammermoor. This lovely aria has abrupt slower tempo passages with the D to high B, etc. and a technical flourish at the end that allows for the aforementioned bravura.

Ah! bello me ritorna (Return to me oh beautiful one, as in the bloom of our true love) from Norma has an even, almost march-like pulse to settle into and it's in the most trumpet-friendly key of our F Major, so a joy to play! In order to feel the spirit of the opera stage, I chose to include not only the full orchestral introduction but also a rather lengthy ending that brings Bellini's proclamation of love aria to a triumphant finality.

Casta Diva, (Chaste Goddess) a true masterpiece by Bellini is also from Norma, an opera which is regarded as a leading example of the Bel Canto genre. **Casta Diva** one of the most famous soprano arias of the 19th century exhibits lyricism at it's very finest, a pensive, minor contrasting section followed by some interesting flourishes before coming to a gentle murmur of a close.

Surta e la notte (Night is approaching) from Ernani has that lilting flowing melody in waltz time that Verdi was so famous for. Note that this aria is number 84 in Arban's The Art of Phrasing in our key of G Major. To get an even deeper understanding of **Surta e La notte,** I recommend you play it in that key, unaccompanied, of course. At the cadenza when playing with the track, try to time it to conclude with the orchestra's resolving chord. I chose to play it freely to keep it in character. As I mentioned earlier, this kind of passage may require several listenings.

Ah! non credea mirarti (Oh, I didn't believe to see you) from Bellini's La Sonnambula is perhaps one of the most beautiful melodies ever written! I know that's sounds like an exaggeration but listen carefully to it's exquisite quality and see if you don't agree. This aria sounds rather simple but is deceptive in that you have to express rather freely yet in sync with the accompaniment. The goal is to create an illusion that they are following you. No easy task but well worth it! I also recommend you go to your Arban book and play it for it's number 111 in The Art of Phrasing in our of key of Bb Major.

Verdi's **Ernani!Ernani,involami** (Ernani!Ernani,save me) is another easily adaptable soprano aria in that if one ignores the operatic context and just gets deeply involved in it's trumpetistic phrases it will feel like home. Certainly it has the challenges that I have spoken about but they are quite natural deviations from a steady pulse and shouldn't present too much of an obstacle.

Addio del passato (Farewell happy dreams of the past) is perfect for the flugelhorn because of its warm and mellow timbre. This poignant aria from Verdi's La Traviata is one of my favorites for it cries out for an emotion drenched performance. Listen, as I did to Maria Callas' 1953 recording on YouTube for inspiration.

L'offeso onor, signori (The offended honor, gentlemen) an aria from Ernani where Silva tells the king and Ernani that he will avenge himself on the two strangers in the company of his bride-to-be. As I said earlier, we instrumentalists need not get that involved with such an emotion but rather enjoy Verdi's fine composition in trumpet fashion. Frankly, I put a considerable amount of "bite" into the articulation in order to convey that I (as Silva) wanted revenge for the dishonor I suffered!

La Traviata is filled with famous tunes and melodies. Alfredo's aria **De miei bollenti spiriti** (Wild my dream of ecstasy) opens the second act of the opera when we find Alfredo and Violetta happily living together. Violetta has abandoned her life as a courtesan and Alfredo could not be any happier because of that. He sings of his happy life with Violetta and how much she loves him. I chose the flugelhorn to express how one feels when life's difficulties have resolved into pleasure and happiness. Verdi's intense accompaniment is filled with a exciting, forward motion that seems to say, the future will be good!

Infelice! E tu credevi (Foolish dreamer! A true believer). We're back into the drama of Ernani with Silva dealing with his offended honor. All that aside, this is a beautiful melody to play on the flugelhorn and when you get to what is a cadenza at the end, I played it in time with just a slight ritardando before the last note.

And now we get to the only aria that is not composed by one of the Italian masters of the Golden Age of Opera. **Ein Mädchen Oder Weibchen** (A Cuddly Wife) from Mozart's The Magic Flute is a bass voice aria for which I found the flugelhorn more in character. Other than having to switch from 2/4 time to 6/8 this should be a relatively easier piece than the others. I discovered in adapting operatic music for trumpet that the bass arias are usually sparse or somewhat transparent in contrast to the tenor and soprano arias which tend to be more complex.

With this album and my previous opera albums, trumpet players have a diverse collection to study and perform not unlike Professor Arban's Art of Phrasing where he included many excerpted operatic arias. The obvious advantage with Music Minus One is you get to enjoy these masterpieces as the composers intended; in great depth and accompanied by a full orchestra!

If you would like a complimentary FaceTime or Skype session where I would be happy to share with you how to get the most benefit from my Music Minus One offerings, you may contact me at bobzottolamusic@comcast.net.

Enjoy!
Bob Zottola, *Naples, Florida*

Giuseppe Verdi

and The Golden Age of Italian Opera

CONTENTS

ISBN 978-1-941566-76-3

MMO 6857

Solo Bb Trumpet or Flugelhorn

Volta la terrea

from *Un Ballo in Maschera*

Giuseppe Verdi
Edited by Robert Zottola

Volta la terrea

Solo Bb Trumpet or Flugelhorn

Quando rapito in estasi

from *Lucia Di Lammermoor*

Gaetano Donizetti
Edited by Robert Zottola

Solo Bb Trumpet or Flugelhorn

Ah! bello mi ritorna

from *Norma*

Vincenzo Bellini
Edited by Robert Zottola

Casta diva

from *Norma*

Solo Bb Trumpet or Flugelhorn

Vincenzo Bellini
Edited by Robert Zottola

Solo Bb Trumpet or Flugelhorn

Surta e la notte
from *Ernani*

Giuseppe Verdi
Edited by Robert Zottola

MMO 6857

Solo Bb Trumpet or Flugelhorn

Ah! non credea mirarti

from *La Sonnambula*

Vincenzo Bellini
Edited by Robert Zottola

Solo Bb Trumpet or Flugelhorn

Ernani! Ernani, involami

from *Ernani*

Giuseppe Verdi
Edited by Robert Zottola

MMO 6857

Solo Flugelhorn

Addio del passato

from *La Traviata*

Giuseppe Verdi
Edited by Robert Zottola

Solo Bb Trumpet or Flugelhorn

L' offeso onor, signori

from *Ernani*

Giuseppe Verdi
Edited by Robert Zottola

MMO 6857

Solo Flugelhorn

De miei bollenti spiriti

from *La Traviata*

Giuseppe Verdi
Edited by Robert Zottola

Solo Flugelhorn

Infelice! E tu credevi

from *Ernani*

Giuseppe Verdi
Edited by Robert Zottola

Solo Flugelhorn

Ein Mädchen oder Wiebchen

from *The Magic Flute*

W.A. Mozart
Edited by Robert Zottola

All Transcriptions by Kevin Mauldin

Music Minus One

50 Executive Boulevard • Elmsford, New York 10523-1325
914-592-1188 • e-mail: info@musicminusone.com
www.musicminusone.com

MMO 6857   ISBN 978-1-941566-76-3